I'll Never Play
the Hammered Dulcimer

poems by

Jan Hanson

Finishing Line Press
Georgetown, Kentucky

I'll Never Play the Hammered Dulcimer

For my family

Copyright © 2019 by Jan Hanson
ISBN 978-1-63534-775-3 First Edition
All rights reserved under International and Pan-American Copyright Conventions. No part of this book may be reproduced in any manner whatsoever without written permission from the publisher, except in the case of brief quotations embodied in critical articles and reviews.

ACKNOWLEDGMENTS

"In Texas" was originally published in *Southwestern American Literature*.

The author is grateful for her husband, who gifted her with her first writing retreat; for the members of Cecilia Woloch's writing workshops; for the Anam Cara Writer's Retreat on the Beara Peninsula in Ireland; and for her teachers: Cecilia Woloch, Leanne O'Sullivan and Lisa Pasold.

Publisher: Leah Maines
Editor: Christen Kincaid
Cover Art: Kimberly L. Jackson
Author Photo: Russell Gearhart
Cover Design: Leah Huete

Printed in the USA on acid-free paper.
Order online: www.finishinglinepress.com
also available on amazon.com

Author inquiries and mail orders:
Finishing Line Press
P. O. Box 1626
Georgetown, Kentucky 40324
U. S. A.

Table of Contents

I
I'll Never Play the Hammered Dulcimer 1
In Texas 2
Floor-Washing Day 3
Sandstorm 4
The Skirt 5
The First Day 6
On a Beach Towel in the Back Yard, 1966 8

II
I Was Young with Him 9
Bolero 11
Year One 12
Evening Beatitude, Florida, 1977 14
The Beginning 15
How Did I Tell Them 16
Garage Sale 17

III
Truman 19
Pale Green Light 20
To All the Men Who Blew It 21

IV
I Am Not a Famous Singer 23
College 24
Apartment 25
Unraveling 26
Final Hours 27
I Used to Wear High Heels 28
The Other Side 29

I.

I'LL NEVER PLAY THE HAMMERED DULCIMER

dressed in flowing calico, my body pulsing,
making music like water dancing on diamonds.

I'll never play the alto recorder,
warming the rosewood in my hands before it transforms
my moist breath into sultry, hollow resonance.

I'll never play the guitar, my long auburn hair brushing
the strings as I strum simple rhythms, singing in Spanish
Adiós a mi Juan, adiós Rosalita.

I'll never play the piano, head bent over the keys,
not looking at sheet music, my fingers knowing where to go.
The way my father played, notes escaping his soul and

finding new life in Dixieland on Sunday mornings while his family
got ready for church. My brothers yelling, my sister crying,
my mother cajoling, me bossing everyone.

Mary Janes and ankle socks, dresses, curlers, clip-on ties,
barrettes, dogs, Wild Root Cream Oil, Aqua Net,
pancakes, bacon, sticky syrup in dishwater.

My dad lost in *Bye, Bye Blues.*

IN TEXAS

At my grandmother's house in Texas,
I wear an organdy pinafore and eat Sunday ham
and Kentucky Wonders off a pink-flowered plate,
swinging my legs under the ladder-back chair.

At my grandmother's house, I am allowed
to sip cream-and-sugar coffee
from her teaspoon.

After dinner, we use bread to sop up gravy
and all the scraps go into a pie tin
for the cats.

My bed for the afternoon is a pallet made of quilts
on the living room floor. My lullaby,
the flutter of the shade in the open window.

FLOOR-WASHING DAY

On floor-washing day,
my mother puts the kitchen chairs
upside down on the gray metal table,
shiny chrome legs point to the ceiling.
My little brother and I climb up into our stagecoach,
holding onto the chair legs as we sway back and forth,
shooting at train robbers.

Roy Rogers gallops alongside,
leaps from his horse,
lands between my brother and me,
grabs the reins and snaps them up and down,
yells at the horses, makes them go faster, faster,
until with one last twist of the mop, gray water
dripping into the bucket, the beige and white linoleum
is clean.

SANDSTORM

Flung by the hot El Paso wind,
sand flies across the schoolyard
in long stinging needles.

I jump and kick so the sand won't find
my bare legs. But it finds my eyes,
it finds my hair. It finds my mouth
when I open it to yell through the shut window
at the sixth grade teacher inside.

Other children run through the dry storm
to waiting quiet cars.

My throat closes.
If I don't have water, I'll die.
They'll find me after the storm
covered with sand near the tetherball pole.

THE SKIRT

Once a week I had to wear
the skirt that looked like a drape,
enormous pink flowers
green leaves and stems

because my mother
had unrolled it from the bath towel
where it had soaked up dampness
from her ritual sprinkling
and ironed it, using long, loving strokes,
heat rising from the board,
Paul Harvey on the radio.

I was twelve,
I did what my mother said.
I put on the skirt and a starched white blouse
clunked my saddle shoes up the steps of the school bus
and sat as small as I could.

THE FIRST DAY

of first grade at my first school,
George R. Bean Elementary, Lubbock, Texas,
my mother brings me to the classroom and leaves me
in front of gawking children who already have places to sit.
The teacher points to a desk in the back of the room.

We move to El Paso in April of the second grade.
On my first day, a boy at the table next to me sneezes,
and a string of green snot comes out of his nose.

On my first day of third grade, I sit on the carpet in front of
the red chenille couch, my mother sits above me,
brushes my hair into a high ponytail.
I walk down Brazos Avenue and turn onto a dirt road,
a dirty white Brahma bull follows me with his eyes.
We are separated by a single strand of barbed wire.

On the first day of fourth grade in Corpus Christi
I wait on the playground of Sam Houston Elementary
in a brown plaid cotton dress, my auburn hair
brushed by my mother from pin curls into fluff around my face,
a hot, sticky wind blowing through me.

On the first day of fifth grade, I stand in the grassy schoolyard
of South Hurst Elementary, another new school in another new town.
Boys play kickball, girls huddle in a privileged circle under an oak tree.
I clutch the brown cloth book bag given to me
by a man who works with my father.

On the first day of sixth grade, I stand on concrete at
White Point Elementary, San Pedro, California.
Past the glimmer of the Pacific Ocean below the school,
I can see the misty outline of Catalina Island.
Girls play hopscotch, the game squares painted
on the cement playground, not etched with a stick

in the dirt, like in Texas. My twangy accent would
make these kids laugh, so I don't speak.

On the first day of seventh grade, at Dana Junior High in San Pedro,
I wait outside the sprawling school for the first class,
a bedlam of Spanish, Portuguese, shouting, banging locker doors
in the open-air hallways. I have friends from last year at White Point,
Barbara, Lynn, Vickie, they find me.
We huddle together until the first bell rings.

On the first day of eighth grade, I am in the kitchen of our
new pink stucco tract house in Orange, California.
We haven't moved in yet, there's no furniture,
the floors are covered with construction dust.
My father has a new job at Disneyland.
He drove me this morning from San Pedro
to the house, not the school, so I will experience
walking to Yorba Junior High like I will every day after this.

My father left me with milk, a box of Grape Nuts, a bowl and a spoon.
I pour Grape Nuts in the bowl and cover them with milk.
The first mouthful brings bile to my throat, and I choke.
I pour the rest into a hole that I dig with the
cereal spoon in the dirt of the back yard.

ON A BEACH TOWEL IN THE BACK YARD, 1966

I lie in the sun on our concrete patio.
Coppertone, milky white, smoothed on my body,
thoughts of salt water, warm sand, smoldering driftwood.
My parents' transistor radio near my head,
"*Boss Radio,*" *93/KHJ*, I wait, wait
for the primeval song to come,
and it does come, pulsing, raw.
Wild thing, you make my heart sing.

Headed down the Newport Freeway to the beach,
my friend Lynette is driving, right hand on the steering wheel,
left arm hanging out the open window in the sun.
Lynette says we have to get a head start on our tan.
I hang my right arm out the window on the other side.

At the beach, we find our friends, our Disneyland co-workers-
Skyway operators, sweepers, food stand cashiers-
always someone I know is there,
always between the volleyball nets and the sea wall,
always a place for me on the sand.

II.

I WAS YOUNG WITH HIM

I turn the key in the door of the apartment
where he sleeps in his single bed,
covered by the old gray cotton quilt
that used to be his mother's.
I lift the quilt and lie down next to him.
I want to tell him about a song I just heard:
You ask me if there'll come a time
when I grow tired of you
Never my love
Never my love

I see a picture of him in the Disneyland employee newsletter,
smiling as he leans over a fence,
chin resting on his folded arms.
I clip it out and put it in my blue vinyl wallet.

On the bus going to Mammoth, he is one seat behind me.
He sings, *when I was seventeen, it was a very good year.*
When he forgets a line, I turn and sing
it was a very good year for city girls
who lived up the stair.

I sit on a splintery bench,
watching him play softball with his team from work,
loving the way the back of his neck
becomes strong and straight when he throws the ball.

I sit across the table from him at
Manny's restaurant, my feet nesting
on top of his. He says he has some shirts
to be ironed. Would I like to iron them?

Would I like to iron his shirts permanently?

Yes, I say, to this proposal of marriage.
We are engaged on my twentieth birthday.
April 8, 1968, we're to be married in the church I grew up in.
There is an earthquake before the ceremony,
jolting me as I apply my mascara in front of
the medicine cabinet mirror.

On a warm Saturday afternoon one year later,
I look out the front door of our house,
my husband tumbles with our puppy
on the fresh-cut lawn; the aroma of the sweet damp grass
entering me each time I breathe.

BOLERO

"A fifteen-minute crescendo," the radio announcer says, as I leave the grocery store parking lot. I'm almost home, but I drive around and around the block as the crescendo builds, and I think of Tom and the first time I heard *Bolero*, lying on the carpet in his apartment in Anaheim with the lid closed on his dark wood console stereo to produce the best sound. He wanted to make love to *Bolero*, and we did, on the floor next to the stereo. A fifteen-minute crescendo.

YEAR ONE

In May, 1969, she was twenty-one years old.
Each week she pored through
The Betty Crocker New Dinner for Two Cookbook,
wrote down dinner menus for a week at a time
and posted them on the refrigerator.

He came home from work
one pot roast Tuesday and said,
"Oh, by the way, I had pot roast for lunch."

Every Saturday afternoon,
he lined up lawn equipment, tools, crates
in the driveway and swept, scrubbed,
while she cleaned the house inside
vacuuming, dusting, stripping wax off linoleum floors.

Afterwards, out for dinner with his friends
and their wives, who were not friends of hers,
he and his pals laughed about high school, the army,
life before marriage.

Sundays, he played golf. She went to church.
Mondays, he went to work as a department manager.
She went to school—to become a teacher,
to contribute to the household income—
when not making curtains for the kitchen windows,
or looking for new dinner recipes, or making macramé hangings
for pots filled with maidenhair fern.

In June, a letter from the university informed her
she was disqualified due to lack of attendance.

Late that afternoon, she left the letter
next to the weekly menu on the refrigerator
and drove around the neighborhood
until she was sure he was home and had read it.

On a Thursday in July,
she went to the doctor for headaches.

"Is everything ok at home?"
She said yes.

I said no.

EVENING BEATITUDE, FLORIDA, 1974

Blessed are houses sprawling wide over Bahia grass,
oak trees with thick trunks, bottom branches low to the ground,
orange trees heavy with fruit.
Blessed are shirtless little boys in cowboy hats
who ride Big Wheels with plastic tires that rumble on the asphalt,
laugh as they chase each other through the grass,
throw fallen oranges like rubber balls.
Blessed are dogs who roam the neighborhood,
licking hands and faces, eating bones and meat scraps tossed in the dirt.
Blessed are women who emerge from houses at dusk
and slap mosquitoes as they gossip in the street before dinner.
Blessed are men in rumpled white shirts, home.

THE BEGINNING

My first poem came to me
on a busy Saturday morning in 1977,
my children's voices coming from the playroom,
Hotel California on the radio, my husband
outside in the driveway washing the car.

I put down the dust cloth,
the yellow can of Lemon Pledge,
sat on the edge of the bed
and wrote *I hear voices nearby
and music, but I am alone...*

I didn't show my poem to my husband.
Why would I, when I could stay warm in my words,
my secret message to myself?

HOW DID I TELL THEM

those two soft children? Did I hold them close
on the brown leather couch and say,
"Your daddy's not going to live with us anymore?"

That's what I heard my daughter, age five, explain to her friend
as they played on the porch and I listened through the front door:
"My daddy's not going to live with us anymore."

And my son, age three, sitting on the floor
near the coffee table in the living room,
tore his straw cowboy hat to pieces.

GARAGE SALE

By noon, the scavengers are gone
and I sit among the leavings.

My Olivetti typewriter, smooth and shiny black,
that used to sit on a wooden stand in the

entryway of our house. His long wooden water skis,
mocking me and my fear of the water.

My patterns in crisp white envelopes,
shirtwaist dresses never made.

His phonograph albums. The Beach Boys, Frank
Sinatra, the Kingston Trio posing in striped shirts

with banjo, guitar and bass. My macramé rope
and beads, projects started but never finished.

His old golf clubs, replaced over the years
several times with the latest models.

My white dress in a box. Simple,
made in Italy, with a hood for a veil.

The red tool box he left when he left, in case
I ever needed a hammer.

III.

TRUMAN

The first boy I remember: Truman Reynolds, fourth grade, Corpus Christi, Texas, 1956. Shorter than I was, a little pudgy, brown hair. Truman "claimed" me. On a field trip to the sea wall in downtown Corpus Christi, he gave me a white football cleat to wear on a chain around my neck. "I claim you," he said. Boys gave girls cleats to establish them as their territory, each color a different level of commitment to their claim. White was marriage, as in, "I'm going to marry you." I was very happy about this recognition, and excited that my future was secure. My family moved away from Corpus Christi at the end of that year. Neither of my husbands were named Truman.

PALE GREEN LIGHT

In the shower, pale green light
filters through frosted window glass
morning after a party night
beautiful warm water flowing
over our shiny, silky bodies
he will leave soon, go home to his wife
I will go teach Sunday school

TO ALL THE MEN WHO BLEW IT

You blew it when you said you didn't want to
be married to me anymore and left our house
with your stereo and your tools and your golf clubs.

You blew it when you got up from my bed, pulled on your jeans
and your Tony Lama cowboy boots and walked out my door.

You blew it when you had your secretary send me a letter
telling me you moved to Atlanta.

You blew it when you told me you regretted
coming to my house in the middle of the night because
you almost got in an accident on the way over and for what?

You blew it when you led me to think that when I got to California
we would have a *relationship*, or would at least *see each other*
to explore whether there would be a relationship,
and then when I got to California, you said you didn't want to see me.

You blew it when you called me and said
you didn't think we were a good match,
even though we conversed with each other
in Spanish, and you wrote poetry to me
and we both had red hair.

You blew it when you wrote me a letter
telling me my children were too important to me.

You blew it when you danced with me in
in the hotel nightclub after the trade show,
and I went with you to your room, and left at dawn,
and you never even asked my name.

IV.

I AM NOT A FAMOUS SINGER

Although, I *am* a singer, alto in the choir, hearing harmony instead of melody. If I were to become famous, I'd have to learn how to sing the melody. I'd have to like accolades, and autograph hounds and people coming up to me in the bathroom saying, "I really loved you in this or that show," and having them try to tell me about how they were going to be a famous singer someday because they're getting an agent and they've got some really great songs they've written and would I like to hear one? If I were a famous singer I'd have to decide where to build my mansion and I'd have to have bodyguards with me all the time and I'd have to memorize all those songs and worry about forgetting the words in front of thousands of people. I'm not a famous singer because I can't hit a note above A or below G, a one-octave range. If you're a famous singer, people have to like hearing you sing.

COLLEGE

My daughter and I laugh in the car
all the way up the 101.
Her bags and TV, stereo and posters
fill the back seat and the trunk.

We climb stairs to take her stuff
to the third floor, second room down.
Nice roommate, pictures of high school life
already on the wall.

That's it, then.
I walk out of the room, down the stairs.
Through my car window, I look to the
third floor up, second window from the end.

Maybe she'll be there, waving.

APARTMENT

When my son was seven, I got him the Atari he wanted
for Christmas. He hadn't told me he wanted it,
but it was there when he snuck into the living room
before dawn on Christmas morning.

When he wanted to join Indian Guides, I went with him
to the orientation meeting, the only mom in the room.

When he wanted to join Cub Scouts, and there was no more
room in the dens, I started a new den and became the
den mother. When he played soccer, I was the team mom
and stayed up until four in the morning making the banner
for the team photo. I took pictures of him trying to score,
and handed out cut-up oranges and Gatorade to the team.

Now, at twenty-three, he says he has found a great apartment
across from Paramount Studios. "If you stand in the middle of the street
and know where to look, you can see the Hollywood sign."

Helping him move in, I scrub the kitchen
starting with the bottom shelves. I make no comment
about the bug droppings and painted-over spaghetti.
I need clean soapy water every few minutes, one bucket after another.

He hangs blinds, hooks up his stereo, and lowers to the floor
the mattress that will be his bed. I make no comment
about the number of locks on the apartment door.
I don't ask about the iron bars that cover the windows.

UNRAVELING

Waking up in the morning is hard, but when it finally happens
I'm glad it does, because if I don't wake up,
I could possibly be dead. Although,
I could also just be wanting to sleep longer
since sleep is so rare, with life crashing in all the time,
work, work, always work, and family, and garages full of stuff
that needs to be gone through but not discarded,
because that's my life thrown on the heap in the dumpster
with the broken stuff and old lamps and boxes and chairs,
like now with my mother's life being gone through
and thrown out without her knowing while she sits
in her mobile home watching the Hour of Power,
all those carefully marked boxes and folded fabric
and plastic flowers and muffin tins that used to produce
wonderful aromas but now are bent and scratched,
proving that even Teflon coating can't protect from
aging or deterioration, which is something I worry about
since I'm deteriorating rapidly and I can't let go of all
that happened to me, because I am what happened to me,
and yet I must move forward, must deteriorate,
must give up my life to those who come after me
for them to throw my things away without me knowing—

or if I'm smart I'll hide my stuff so they can't find it,
since I wouldn't want them to really know me anyway.

FINAL HOURS

Sunlight bathes my mother
as she lies in the hospital bed near the window
of the small bedroom in our home.
She is covered by the Dresden plate quilt
her mother-in-law made on a frame
set up in her Texas living room. Circles of fabric,
scraps from my blue seersucker Easter dress,
my brother's red plaid cotton shirt.
My mother and my grandmother did not get along.
They quarreled over which way the toilet paper
should come off the roll, and whether a five-year-old
child should be allowed to sip coffee from a teaspoon.

We've hired Yolanda to care for our mother,
and she does, as if she were her own mother,
as I should be caring for my own mother,
the work I can't do, the turning of the frail body,
the cleaning of the soiled linens,
the changing of the gown.

I want my mother to have licorice
like on her birthday every year,
we all knew she loved it and we tucked
a bit into whatever presents we gave.
I buy licorice now, and cut it into pieces
the size of peppercorns and smash it
between two spoons with warm water
to melt it and make it soft so she can taste the
musky sweetness.

I put the spoon to her dry lips
and she blinks, and whimpers,
please, Mom, please taste it
please like it
please remember licorice

I USED TO WEAR HIGH HEELS

In the doctor's office waiting room
I look up at the sound of a woman's high heels
clicking across the linoleum.
I look down at my flat, soft scruffy black shoes
that make no important sound when I walk.

I used to wear high heels.
So high that my legs in their taupe stockings
felt long and capable as they took me
from my office to meetings and training presentations
where I would be the one up front, speaking to the group,
pointing to topics on flip charts
that I prepared in advance using
Magic Markers in many colors
for emphasis.

"Good morning, everyone. Today we are going to talk about…"
Effective Communication Techniques
Conflict Resolution
Building Exceptional Teams
Leading and Managing in the 90s

People came to me for answers.
Vice presidents asked my opinion.
They gave me promotions and raises and new titles.
Everyone knew who I was.

THE OTHER SIDE

> *Praise God! I feel like singing. I'm on the other side of life now.*
> Alan O'Bryant

From the other side of life, it might seem that
I was not happy with my life on earth.
On earth, I wrote about divorce, death, regret,
anger, pain, revenge, disappointment.
Why was my writing so hopeless?

Did I not see my granddaughter's face
when I went to visit on Sunday afternoons?
Or hear her laugh, or feel her arms
around my neck?

Did I not feel the crunch of seed pods under my feet,
dropped from the tree in our front yard onto the sidewalk?
Or look up through the branches of that tree and see
first green, then blue, then green again
as the soft breeze moved its leaves?

Did I not hear, as I sat reading in our back yard,
the hum of a lawn mower in the distance,
the bell-ring from the school around the corner,
an airplane flying low over our house?

Did I not see our blue and white kitchen,
sun through the skylight,
yellow dishtowel hanging on the oven door,
the note my mother put in my lunchbox
in September, 1954, framed in the window?

To our big girl on her first day at school,
we hope you have many, many happy times here.

J an Hanson has more than 30 years of experience writing in the business world, while writing poetry in a parallel universe. Her earliest business writing experience was as an eligibility worker for the department of social services, where hand-writing narratives documenting contact with clients was a daily requirement. Her work as advertising coordinator for a cattleman's association publication brought new opportunities for written communication. And her decades-long career in human resources saw the evolution from formal letter-writing and file documentation hammered out on a Selectric typewriter, to complex and detailed electronic documentation of all manner of investigations and complaints. In school, she studied organizational development, which gave her tools for a successful career. But it was what she experienced in writing workshops—held in living rooms, sun porches, and small gatherings under pine trees—that made poetry happen.

www.ingramcontent.com/pod-product-compliance
Lightning Source LLC
LaVergne TN
LVHW040117080426
835507LV00041B/1509